Stressed Out!

Michelle R. Prather

Consultants

Diana Herweck, Psy.D.
Clinical Director

Publishing Credits

Rachelle Cracchiolo, M.S.Ed., *Publisher*
Conni Medina, M.A.Ed., *Managing Editor*
Nika Fabienke, Ed.D., *Series Developer*
June Kikuchi, *Content Director*
John Leach, *Assistant Editor*
Lee Aucoin, *Senior Graphic Designer*

TIME For Kids and the TIME For Kids logo are registered trademarks of TIME Inc. Used under license.

Image Credits: Cover and p.1 JGI/Jamie Grill/Getty Images; p.4 Paul D. Stewart/Science Source; all other images from iStock and/or Shutterstock

Library of Congress Cataloging-in-Publication Data

Names: Prather, Michelle Rene?e, 1975- author.
Title: Life in numbers : stressed out! / Michelle R. Prather, M.A.
Description: Huntington Beach, CA : Teacher Created Materials, [2017] |
  Audience: Grade 4 to 6. | Includes index.
Identifiers: LCCN 2017017376 (print) | LCCN 2017030555 (ebook) | ISBN
  9781425853587 (eBook) | ISBN 9781425849849 (pbk.)
Subjects: LCSH: Stress in children--Juvenile literature.
Classification: LCC BF723.S75 (ebook) | LCC BF723.S75 P73 2017 (print) | DDC
  155.4/189042--dc23
LC record available at https://lccn.loc.gov/2017017376

Teacher Created Materials
5301 Oceanus Drive
Huntington Beach, CA 92649-1030
http://www.tcmpub.com
ISBN 978-1-4258-4984-9
© 2018 Teacher Created Materials, Inc.

Table of Contents

What Is Stress?.. 4

Are You Stressed Out? 6

Stress Affects Health 18

Put a Stop to Stress... 24

Glossary 28

Index... 29

Check It Out! 30

Try It!.. 31

About the Author 32

What Is Stress?

It is unusual to go a day without hearing someone talk about being stressed. Maybe a parent mentions during dinner that a big work project has been "very stressful." Or you and your friends worry about an upcoming math test. Stress is the body's reaction to certain situations and feelings. It changes how the body functions and how you feel about life—at least temporarily.

Stress sounds…well, stressful! But stress is a normal part of your day, and you should not be afraid of it. Stress can help you protect yourself from threatening **circumstances** and get things done. But too much stress can wear out your body and mind.

Prehistoric Stress

Our ancestors often crossed paths with wild animals. This stress sent adrenaline through their bodies. The adrenaline helped them quickly decide if they should fight or run away.

Such a Rush

Adrenaline is one of the hormones released into your bloodstream when you are under pressure. It makes your heart beat faster and your blood pressure rise. It gives you a rush of energy, too.

Are You Stressed Out?

Every day, you **confront** a variety of things that cause stress, even if you do not realize it. You might be unsure of what you are feeling at first. But pay close attention to your body's reactions. These signs can help you **gauge** your stress levels in different situations.

Imagine that you have to present an oral report. If you feel relaxed and confident, you might also feel happy. You know you will get a good grade. Your body and mind feel peaceful. On the other hand, you are definitely *not* at peace if thinking about the report gives you a headache. Signs of stress might include a racing heart, weak knees, or **nausea** (NAH-zhuh).

Fighting Stress

Everyone reacts to stress differently. When you start to experience signs of stress, take slow, deep breaths. Focus on calming images. This will distract your mind and help your body calm down.

The State of Stress

If you find yourself feeling stressed a lot, you are not alone. Many kids are often stressed. One report showed that almost one-third of kids suffered a health problem due to stress in the last month.

Your Body on Stress

Stress can affect your body from head to toe. People who are very sensitive to stress can feel several **symptoms** all at once. Others might feel only one or two. The symptoms can come and go, or they can last until the stressful event has passed.

Some of these pesky red flags your body raises can feel like a cold or the flu. But it is a good idea to ask yourself: "Could I be stressed, rather than sick?" Talk to a parent or guardian about whether you should see a doctor.

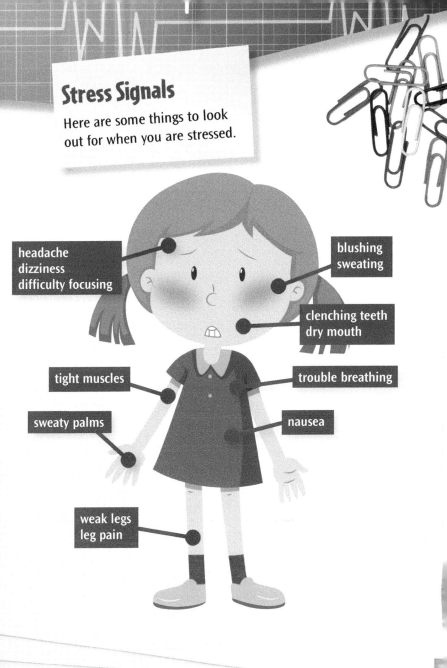

Stress Signals

Here are some things to look out for when you are stressed.

headache
dizziness
difficulty focusing

blushing
sweating

clenching teeth
dry mouth

tight muscles

trouble breathing

sweaty palms

nausea

weak legs
leg pain

Measuring Your Mood

There is a handy way to take note of how stressed you are. You can use a number scale just like **psychologists** (sy-KAW-luh-jihsts) who study stress. The scale goes from 1 to 10.

If you are feeling nearly stress-free, you would rate yourself at 1. If you rate yourself between 4 and 7, you are having a stressful day, but this is still in the "normal" range. If your stress level is 8, 9, or 10, you need to take a break. Your body is working overtime to combat the stress. Get some fresh air, stretch your muscles, or talk to a trusted friend. You need to relax in order to function normally again.

The Stress Hormone

Cortisol is a hormone that your body releases when you are stressed. It gives your body a burst of glucose, or sugar. This provides energy. But constant stress creates too much of this hormone— and it could start working against you.

LOW NORMAL HIGH

CORTISOL

Going with the Flow

When stress makes your heart race, your entire body gets in on the act. Your breathing is faster, and your lungs take in more oxygen. Blood flow can increase three to four times!

Stress Level: 1–3

Stress Level: 4–7

Stress Level: 8–10

School Stress

Kids spend much of their time at school. This is where a lot of stress can occur. Friendships and grades are often in **flux** and can set off the stress alarm. Being bullied can make you lose sleep at night. Always tell a teacher or another trusted adult if you feel scared or anxious at school.

Things that happen at school can affect you all day, even if they do not seem like a big deal at the time. You might come home from school feeling angry, but you do not know why. Take some time to write or draw about your feelings. When you are able to think a little bit more clearly, talk to an adult about what is bothering you.

Bullying

Bullying can make you feel stressed and scared. It includes repeated pushing, hitting, and teasing. Leaving someone out of a game or starting rumors are also forms of bullying. Bullying is never OK.

Truth about Bullying

Students in grades 4 through 12 were surveyed about bullying. About half of them had been bullied at school at least once in the past month. And about one-third said they had bullied others at school.

Home Stress

Home is the other place where you probably spend a lot of your time. Even the happiest households have stressful moments. Running late for school or juggling homework and chores can make you tense. A new baby, or even a puppy, can cause stress. Suddenly, what used to be a calm environment is now more exciting…and more stressful!

Just as you cannot control what is happening in the world, you cannot always control what happens in your life. Moving to a new home can throw you off course. Maybe your parents argue a lot, were recently divorced, or are very worried about money. These things, along with everyday events, can create stress.

Stress Survey

Kids between the ages of 8 and 12 were asked about the things in life that cause them stress. Getting along with a sibling caused stress for 14 out of 100 kids. And 28 out of 100 kids said their stress came from worrying about money.

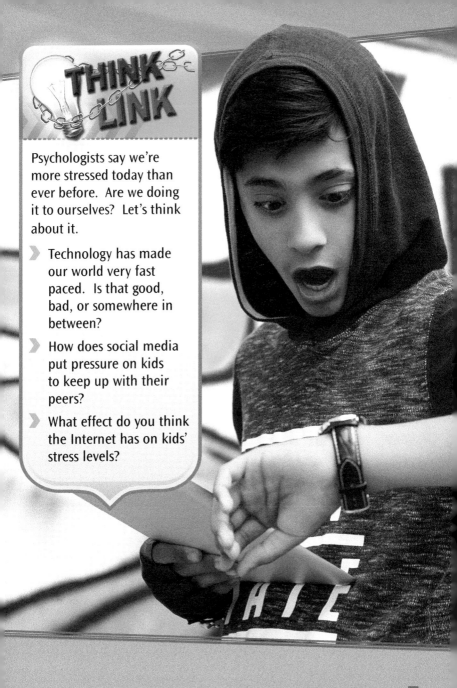

THINK LINK

Psychologists say we're more stressed today than ever before. Are we doing it to ourselves? Let's think about it.

⟩ Technology has made our world very fast paced. Is that good, bad, or somewhere in between?

⟩ How does social media put pressure on kids to keep up with their peers?

⟩ What effect do you think the Internet has on kids' stress levels?

Life Stress

As you grow up, it becomes more common for the world's problems to **seep** into your life. You hear or read about events in the news, and you're aware of more than you were when you were younger. All this new knowledge can begin to weigh you down and make you feel stressed.

It is important to talk to an adult if you are scared about what is going on in the world. Adults can help you understand these events. They can explain why these things are happening. They might even help you think about ways you can change the world for the better!

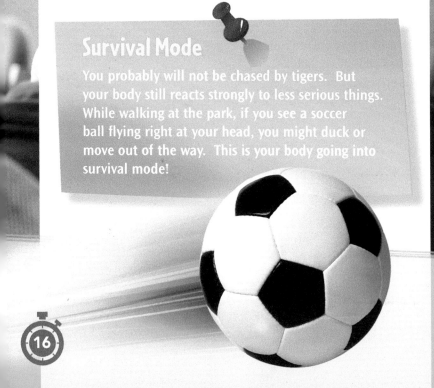

Survival Mode

You probably will not be chased by tigers. But your body still reacts strongly to less serious things. While walking at the park, if you see a soccer ball flying right at your head, you might duck or move out of the way. This is your body going into survival mode!

Getting Along

Some things are more important to you than others—at least for now. Only 1 out of 20 kids ages 8 to 12 were stressed about their future after graduation from high school. But 4 out of 20 was stressed about their friendships.

Stress Affects Health

Everyone reacts to stress differently. But one thing is certain: too much stress can disrupt the balance of your life. From the time you wake up to the time you fall asleep, being on edge affects your mood.

Losing sleep is one **consequence** of too much stress, and this can become a big problem. If you can't turn off your brain at night, you will not get enough sleep. Without the right amount of sleep, you wake up in a fog. It is harder to remember and cope with things. Paying attention in class and focusing become more difficult, too.

The Right Amount

Want to feel fresh and focused every morning? Doctors agree that the way to do it is to get plenty of sleep! Kids ages 6 to 12 should get 9 to 12 hours of sleep every night.

Tired of It

A study of kids ages 8 to 12 showed some facts about sleep. Around 40 out of 100 had a hard time sleeping. But only 13 out of 100 parents knew that their kids had issues with sleep.

There is also a good chance that your daily nutrition will suffer if you are under too much stress. If stress is making you feel sick to your stomach, you likely will not want to eat. So your first **instinct** at mealtime might be to eat very little or to skip eating.

Sometimes, your stomach may respond to stress in the exact opposite way. A lot of people, kids included, eat when they feel anxious, mad, or even too tired. And most of the time, the food used to "feed the problem" is not healthy. Your body probably will not feel so great after eating all that food. Then, your mind might start to feel bad about it, too. Now you're stressed again!

The Sugar Spike

You now know that your body releases adrenaline and cortisol when it is stressed. Those two hormones make your blood sugar go way up and then way down. After a stressful event, you might feel tired. This is an effect of your blood-sugar levels dropping.

Emotional Eating

Eating while stressed is often called *emotional eating*. Reports say some kids as young as 5 years old head straight for treats to help ease their minds.

Control Your Emotions

It is bad enough when stress affects how you feel. When the way you feel changes how you treat other people, it can cause a different kind of stress. Many kids become moody or start talking back at home when they are under too much pressure. If your parents do not know about your stress, they might scold you for being rude. This could upset you and cause you to talk back even more.

You may even find that your friends suddenly annoy you. You might feel **short-tempered** and mean. Or you may feel so sad that you do not want to hang around the people who usually make you happy.

When you are feeling stressed, take a deep breath and think before you speak. Sometimes, it is best to calmly ask for some time alone. That way, you can get your feelings under control before you say something you might regret.

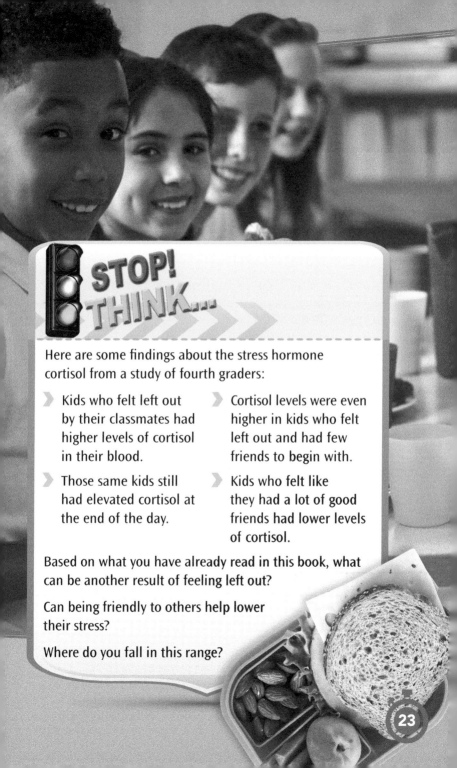

STOP! THINK...

Here are some findings about the stress hormone cortisol from a study of fourth graders:

> Kids who felt left out by their classmates had higher levels of cortisol in their blood.

> Cortisol levels were even higher in kids who felt left out and had few friends to begin with.

> Those same kids still had elevated cortisol at the end of the day.

> Kids who felt like they had a lot of good friends had lower levels of cortisol.

Based on what you have already read in this book, what can be another result of feeling left out?

Can being friendly to others help lower their stress?

Where do you fall in this range?

Put a Stop to Stress

Here is the good news: you can stop stress before it gets to you. There are plenty of activities that can **alleviate** stress. Take a walk around your neighborhood with a friend or parent. Listen to music, play an instrument, or do some crafting. Play a game, run in place, or have a dance party in your living room. Or just do something nice for someone. All these activities help by taking your mind off of whatever is making you stressed!

Try learning about deep breathing and **meditation**. When you breathe from your stomach, your heart rate decreases. By slowing down, you can start to relax. *Aahhh!*

School Meditation

Students at a Maryland school have a special room where they can go when they are feeling stressed. The "Meditation Room" is a quiet place where kids can stretch, do yoga, and calm down.

Scrunch Up Stress!

Grab a magazine or newspaper from your recycling bin and get to work relieving stress. Assign a worry or **woe** to each page, and then crumple it up. Imagine you are throwing that stress away as you toss each ball back into the recycle bin.

Enough Is Enough!

Now that you know stress can be squashed, it is a good time to make this promise. Tell yourself, "Stress will not get the best of me."

You will always have to deal with minor stresses. Your heart will still beat more quickly if you see a strange dog running toward you, and your face may still feel hot and get sweaty when you are embarrassed. But now you know some strategies you can use to overcome stress.

The more we learn about coping with stress, the better we will get along. Imagine if we all took a few deep breaths more often. We would be a happier, healthier, and more peaceful society.

Quiet Time

Schools around the world are starting to take stress seriously. Some have even provided two periods of quiet time each school day. Kids in those schools have better grades and attendance than they did before having quiet time.

Work It Out

Exercise is one great way to relieve stress. And it helps keep your body healthy, too. Exercising is good for your body and your mind, so get active!

Glossary

alleviate—make something less painful or troubling

circumstances—conditions

confront—to face something or somebody; to come up against

consequence—the result of something

flux—a constant state of change

gauge—to figure out and make a judgment about something

instinct—a behavior that is automatic

meditation—the act of clearing the mind in a quiet setting

nausea—the feeling of needing to vomit

psychologists—experts in behavior and the mind

seep—to pass slowly through something

short-tempered—easily made angry

symptoms—signs of something bad

woe—something that causes a problem

Index

adrenaline, 4–5, 20

blood pressure, 5

bullying, 12–13

cortisol, 10, 20, 23

deep breathing, 6, 22, 24, 26

divorce, 14

emotional eating, 21

energy, 5, 10

friends, 4, 10, 12, 17, 22–24

heart, 5–6, 11, 24, 26

home, 14, 22

hormones, 5, 20

Internet, 15

meditation, 24

money, 14

mood, 10, 18, 22

moving, 14

nutrition, 20

oxygen, 11

quiet time, 26

school, 12–14, 24, 26

siblings, 14

sleep, 12, 18–19

social media, 15

symptoms (of stress), 8–9

technology, 15

Check It Out!

Books

Lynch, Christopher. 2012. *Totally Chill: My Complete Guide to Staying Cool.* AAPC Publishing.

Moss, Wendy L. 2015. *Bounce Back: How to Be a Resilient Kid.* Magination Press.

Romain, Trevor, and Elizabeth Verdick. 2005. *Stress Can Really Get on Your Nerves!* Free Spirit Publishing.

Shapiro, Lawrence E., and Robin K. Sprague. 2009. *The Relaxation and Stress Reduction Workbook for Kids: Help for Children to Cope with Stress, Anxiety, and Transitions.* Instant Help.

Websites

Common Sense Media. "Meditation Apps for Kids." www.commonsensemedia.org/lists /meditation-apps-for-kids.

PBS Kids. "It's My Life." www.pbskids.org /itsmylife/.

Try It!

Do you feel lower, grumpier, or more stressed than usual? Figure out what is going on by keeping a log! Log the low parts of your day, and write the best word to describe how you feel. This can help you see the big picture. Writing down the time of day is also useful. That way, you can look for patterns about when you are being pushed to your limit. After keeping a log for a while, you may notice a decrease in your times of stress. If not, go back to pages 24 and 25 for some handy tips on how to relax.

Here is a sample chart to give you an idea of how to start your log:

What Bugged Me Today		
Time	**What Happened**	**I Felt...**
6:30 a.m.	I spilled my cereal.	worried/frustrated
9:00 a.m.	I realized I forgot my math homework.	panicked
10:30 a.m.	Ian bragged about his new phone.	jealous
12:30 p.m.	Tatiana made fun of me in front of everyone.	angry/embarrassed
3:00 p.m.	Dad was late to pick me up.	anxious
6:00 p.m.	I still wasn't finished with homework.	tired/frustrated

About the Author

Michelle R. Prather is a longtime writer and editor. She got her start interviewing business owners and telling their stories in magazines. Since then, she has written guided planners and journals, edited young adult novels, and coauthored an art book. She started college as a dance major, but she ended up with degrees in film studies and history. Her big dreams include opening the best-ever children's bookstore and writing a fiction series her daughter would love.